Pebble® Plus

Pet Questions and Answers

PET FISH

Questions and Answers

by Christina Mia Gardeski

raintree

a Capstone company — publishers for children

Raintree is an imprint of Capstone Global Library Limited, a company incorporated in England and Wales having its registered office at 264 Banbury Road, Oxford, OX2 7DY – Registered company number: 6695582

www.raintree.co.uk
myorders@raintree.co.uk

Edited by Carrie Braulick Sheely and Michelle Hasselius
Designed by Kayla Rossow
Picture research by Pam Mitsakos
Production by Gene Bentdahl

ISBN 978 1 4747 2140 0 (hardback)
20 19 18 17 16
10 9 8 7 6 5 4 3 2 1

ISBN 978 1 4747 2152 3 (paperback)
21 20 19 18 17
10 9 8 7 6 5 4 3 2 1

British Library Cataloguing in Publication Data
A full catalogue record for this book is available from the British Library.

Acknowledgements
Alamy Images: roger askew, 21; Shutterstock: AndreJakubik, 5, carnival, 9, Moo teaforthree, 17, Nikiparonak, 1, 22, Nipon Laicharoenchokchai, 11, oksankash, 19, Pavel Vakhrushev, cover, Photoman29, 13, S-F, 15, voylodyon, 7

Printed and bound in China.

Contents

Who can breathe under water?

My fish! Fish breathe through gills. Water carries gas called oxygen to the gills. The oxygen goes into the blood and through the fish's body. Fish need oxygen to live.

gill

How do fish swim?

Fish wave their bodies back
and forth to swim. Their tail fin
pushes them through the water.
Other fins help them to turn or stop.

tail fin

Can fish smell?

Fish smell through two small holes on their heads. Water flows fast through these holes. The smells in the water tell a fish if food or danger is near by.

Do fish have ears?

Fish do not have ears on their heads.

They have ear parts inside their bodies.

Fish have lines on their sides called cells.

These cells help the fish to know when

something moves near by.

What do fish eat?

Pet fish eat fish flakes or frozen
food made from plants and
animals. Do not feed your fish
too much! This will make the fish ill.
It also makes the water dirty.

Where can I keep my fish?

Pet fish live in fish tanks
filled with water. A pump
keeps the water moving.
A filter keeps the water clean.

Do fish sleep?

Fish do not sleep like humans or other animals. They rest and save energy. Some fish settle down at the bottom of a tank. Other fish float in one spot.

Can I train my fish?

Most fish are clever.

They can be trained to do

simple tricks. Some fish will

swim through hoops for treats.

Can I handle my fish?

Do not handle your fish. You may
hurt it. Your hands can make
the water dirty. Enjoy your
fish from outside its home.

Glossary

energy strength to do active things without getting tired

filter machine that cleans liquids or gases as they pass through it; a filter cleans the water in a fish tank

fin body part that fish use to swim and steer in water

flake small, thin piece of something

gill body part on the side of a fish; fish use their gills to breathe

handle pick up with your hands

oxygen colourless gas; humans and animals need oxygen to breathe

Read more

Fish (Animal Classification), Angela Royston (Raintree, 2015)

Fish Body Parts (Animal Body Parts), Clare Lewis (Raintree, 2015)

Goldie's Guide to Caring for your Fish (Pets' Guides), Anita Ganeri (Raintree, 2015)

Websites

www.bbc.co.uk/nature/animals/by/fish
Discover more about all types of fish.

www.dkfindout.com/uk/animals-and-nature/pet-care
Find out more about pet care.

Comprehension questions

1. Explain how fish breathe.

2. Fish tanks have filters. What are filters?

3. How do fish rest?

Index